THE ALTAR

A true story of faith, love, life and death

Nichola Williams

Published by Good Grounds Media LTD®

ISBN 978-0-9928873-0-8

Cover design and images by Good Grounds Media LTD®

Dedicated to Nanny and the family

You are all such blessings to me. This book is my perspective and experience of a time that affected us all.

Love you lots

To God,

I thank you for never giving up on me, for your awesome ability to get my attention, and for your wonderful gift of Jesus Christ through whom all are saved.

Acknowledgements

Pastor Joseph and my Christian Life Fellowship Family

Pastor Philip and Sheron Ankrah
Jean Marc and Marcia Aka-Kadjo
The members of Good Grounds Life group (2006-2007)

Thank you for your amazing faith in the saviour Jesus Christ, countless prayers, words of encouragement and priceless friendship.

Neala Okuromade - Author of the book 'What's your financial Gameplan?'

Thank you for lending your time to mentor me, sharing your advice and words of wisdom.

To my husband Harold Williams.

You have been such a support during a very difficult time. You are destined for greatness and I am honoured to walk with you in all God has for you. - m.i.n.e

Contents

Introduction

The Lord is not slow in keeping His promise, as some understand slowness. He is patient with you, not wanting anyone to perish but everyone to come to repentance.

2 Peter 3:9 NIV

The one I have come to know as Almighty God is as steadfast as ever. When I ponder all I have experienced with Him it surpasses anything I could have imagined. He has, and continues to go to great lengths to have a relationship with me. His very nature means that He will stop at nothing to keep mankind from eternal death. He longs for the love relationship He intended with us from the beginning of time. This book is a recount of a series of amazing events I experienced with Him over a two-year period, through which my walk with Him changed forever.

Many Christians have had countless prayers answered, witnessed and performed great miracles and experienced victory in their lives. Unfortunately they rarely share such things with others. Our churches may be filled with people whose hearts are willing to go after God but in reality they are finding it hard to stay on course. This could be through a lack of motivation and can be especially true for those who are new in the faith. These individuals can be greatly encouraged by hearing of our experiences and encounters with God.

In the Bible the gospel of Mark challenges us to share the good news with others but what exactly is the good news? The Bible teaches us that Jesus is the Son of God who paid a huge price for all mankind in a master plan of redemption. However we must not forget that Jesus rose again and sent the Holy Spirit to be actively involved in our daily lives. Part of the good news is what we have personally experienced with Him. How has he touched our lives? What has He changed for us? How are things different to before we knew Him? Our lives have silently been changed and that is exactly what happened to me. God did an awesome thing in my life and I have kept quiet about it for several years. This is an opportunity for me to shout loud about the greatness of God and how amazing He actually is.

My husband regularly teaches that we are to build altars in our lives like the saints in the Old Testament. Traditionally an Altar was a place assigned to give a sacrifice. That sacrifice was usually offered to solemnize a covenant or treaty and symbolised a positive relationship between two people or parties. An altar was also built as a reminder of what God had done in the lives of people or nations. In the world today we do all sorts of things to commemorate special events or anniversaries. We hold parties, have plaques laid or hold festivals to remember significant phases of life. An Altar is something that commemorates our encounters with God. It symbolises a place where we last met Him, where we last experienced Him. It serves as a reminder of how God touches our lives and longs to keep us in pursuit of Him.

I was amazed how some of the details of this testimony began to get cloudy. So in addition to the details written in my journals, I jotted down the key events before they were gone. The lasting impact this time in my life has had for me is priceless and I have a beautiful reminder that will remain for years to come.

Everything I have written is as accurate as I remember it to be. I pray that through this book your lives will be blessed. I pray it will draw you nearer to God, causing you to surrender your entire being to Jesus and be a light in the face of a very dark world.

This is my Altar -x-

1

Can I have your attention?

There the angel of the LORD appeared to him in
flames of fire from within a bush. Moses saw that
though the bush was on fire it did not burn up. So
Moses thought, "I will go over and see this strange
sight—why the bush does not burn up."
Exodus 3:2-3 NIV

Dreaming is something that we have all
experienced at some point in our times of sleep.
But from as far back as I can remember mine
have been very detailed. I come from a family of
dreaming women but somehow the vividness and
accuracy that mine had caused people to pay
attention. I would often dream of events before
they happened which perplexed my parents who
put it down to some sort of God-given gift. I did
not understand it myself either and would
regularly struggle with frightening warning
dreams. I grew up in the Methodist Church
which provided a great Christian foundation but I
did not truly come to know God until my late
teens. From this point onwards dreaming became
something that God used quite regularly to
communicate with me. One morning in
September 2006, after getting a good night's

sleep I awoke and recalled having the following dream:

I lay on a hospital bed with several doctors surrounding me discussing the state of my condition. I was undergoing a heart operation, void of pain but somehow aware of everything that was going on. I lay there as they stitched me up and upon completion was transferred to the patient recovery unit to rest. I was still numb from the anaesthetic but could see and hear the doctors discussing how the operation had not been successful. I overheard the female doctor, who stood with a concerned look on her face say that I did not have long left to live. The dream then switched and I no longer lay on the hospital bed. I was now somehow the one looking at the patient, who on closer inspection I recognised as my elderly grandfather. I had a very close relationship with Sidney George Grey, my maternal grandfather and visited him often. He had always been a big part of my childhood and though a man of few words he somehow always communicated that he loved me greatly. I am not sure what exactly he did to communicate this to me; perhaps it was just his very caring temperament and constant willingness to give of himself. He lay there on the hospital bed lifeless, except for his chest moving up and down due to his breathing. I leaned in and began to whisper to him. Speaking very calmly I began to tell him about Jesus and all He had done for mankind and indeed for Grandad. I presented him with the option to surrender his heart to Jesus Christ and accept Him as his personal Lord and Saviour before it was too late. As I prayed what I knew to be the sinner's prayer he was too weak to respond orally instead gently nodding in acknowledgement.

I awoke.

There is usually an initial emotion upon waking which can later serve as an indication to the meaning of my dream. In this instance my initial feeling was definitely one of urgency. Because I dream so frequently I have developed a habit of writing the details down as soon after waking as possible. If not I am likely to forget significant details as my day progresses. In addition to writing a recount (especially for the ones with such detail) I pray and ask God about it and this time I did the same. Somehow I knew that this dream was not about my own health but waited in anticipation of what reply I would get. Slowly I wrote down all God said to me. He told me that

The Altar

Grandad was going to die and that it simply was his time to go. That I should not pray for healing because it was his time to go home instead I should pray for his salvation. God wanted Grandad to surrender his heart to Him so he could spend eternity with Him and was planning to use me in the process. He told me that He loved Grandad very much and had been calling him to draw nearer for quite a long time.

What a way to get my attention! Send me a vividly clear dream along with a simple explanation. God always remains faithful in communicating things with us that need urgent attention. As I tried my best to comprehend what I thought was very sad news, I felt the soft comfort of God's voice as he whispered the words of 2 Peter 3:9:

The Lord is not slow in keeping his promise, as some understand slowness. He is patient with you, not wanting anyone to perish but everyone to come to repentance.

That was the moment I made a decision to stand on God's word and pray earnestly on behalf of my lovely Grandad. Like Moses and the burning bush God had successfully grabbed my attention and with great importance it weighed very heavily on my heart. As I thought about my character flaws and remembered my own failings I felt completely unqualified for the job that awaited me. It is interesting because Moses did the same thing. He questioned God about whether he was the right man too. But God spoke words of assurance and told me that I may be the only one who Grandad will listen to so he counted on me to deliver His word. As much as I felt unprepared, I began to embrace what God had said. Surely He knew what was best and Grandad was worth it. In the next few weeks I prayed for him daily and then frequently throughout the following months. However it would play out, I knew that the salvation of a man, who was known to the King of kings and the Lord of lords, was of great importance.

2

Standing firm

Therefore put on the full armor of God, so that when the day of evil comes, you may be able to stand your ground, and after you have done everything, to stand.
Ephesians 6:13 NIV

As time went by God began to give me more details about Grandad through further dreams, even telling me who I should enlist to pray for him. The thought of sharing such an idea with people was a little nerve-racking, as I did not know how they would respond. How could I be 100% sure enough of what I had heard? And so much so that I share it with others? Surely they would think I was a little crazy or perhaps I had interpreted the dream wrongly? Were the words I claimed to hear from God really from Him? After deciding that this whole topic was going to have to be a faith based one, I plucked up enough courage to begin sharing it with those the Lord put on my heart. I told my husband first, whom I think was rather excited, then two of my younger sisters who were a bit scared. I also told a few close friends who all agreed to join with me in prayer. At this time Grandad's health didn't seem to decline very much and I wavered, sometimes asking myself how much of what I heard may actually be true. Despite this, I continued to pray and whenever I would ease up a bit or succumb to doubt, God would send me another dream. I remember one in which a large angel appeared in the sky above Grandad's home. It repeatedly blew a loud trumpet in the sky as if sending out some sort of message. What looked like sound waves rippled through the sky and I saw Grandad getting carried up by another two angels through the clouds – he was being called home. In a different dream an eagle flew down from heaven to give Grandad a letter. As he read it he responded by stepping out of his kitchen window and flying away. There were lots of others involving packing suitcases for a journey, boarding a train bound for heaven and the harvesting of people, Grandad featured of course. These dreams I experienced all confirmed what God had already communicated and signified that the time was drawing nearer for him to go home.

The start of 2007 was to mark the beginning of a very challenging time concerning the salvation of Grandad. As I soldiered on in prayer, I would frequently experience rather intense spiritual attacks. For many Christians this is a common reality and I was no exception. Scripture tells us that we have an adversary who tries to stop us from doing what God desires and I felt like I was definitely on his radar. At times I felt like giving up, especially since Grandad was still relatively healthy with little complications. Waking up during the night and having to address a spiritual presence was a very common reality. One night I remember such an attack very vividly.

I decided to have an early night on this particular evening and found myself in bed before midnight for once. Long after everyone else had fallen asleep I lay down and was somewhere in between deep sleep and wakefulness. As I lay there I heard my front door being opened by a group of individuals who were bickering loudly (my bedroom is the first room you meet when you enter my house). Lying down still half asleep I listened to the footsteps that had entered my home. After the group stepped in, they walked through the hallway and passed my bedroom whilst the arguing and bickering became louder. It was clear that they were disagreeing on something. I watched them pass my open bedroom door then they entered the next room, which belonged to my children. The arguing continued whilst the children slept soundly. Clearly there seemed to be an issue amongst them about how they ought to carry out whatever they had set out to do. For a moment I felt extremely scared but then quickly got very angry and jumped up out of bed. Since becoming a parent I have found that when it comes to the care and wellbeing of my children I can experience a sense of anger unlike any other time. No demonic power was going to touch even the hairs on my children's heads! I began praying in tongues loudly upon entering the bedroom but found no physical beings only sensed a strong demonic presence. I prayed over my children, not really caring whether I would wake them up. Fortunately they did not stir at all so I anointed them with oil, returned to bed and slept soundly for the rest of the night. In the morning neither my husband nor children had any idea of the events that had occurred that night.

A terrible fear would come over me at times, especially after I had spent some powerful time in prayer. Because I did not know exactly when and how Grandad would leave this Earth, I worried whether things would go smoothly. What if he died before he had a chance to surrender his life? What if I was not around during his last moments? What if I left things too late and he went to hell instead of heaven? Or what if everything I had dreamt was a bunch of nonsense and I had imagined it all? Could I be sure that the dream was indeed from God? All these thoughts entered my mind at some point. God had always been faithful to any word that He had spoken over me so I had a deep knowing that He would not let me down this time. He never had. I could only trust Him.

Many a frightening encounter was to be my experience through this battle and when I was not facing attack, my young family seemed to be on the end of it. I remember when I began to develop horribly painful bruises along the front of both legs. I had never experienced anything like this before but it started out with one or two normal looking bruises. I assumed that these were a result of bumping into something or playing rough with my sons but as time progressed I realized that it must be something else. I began to develop a few more bruises everyday for about a week before I decided that it would be best for me to seek advice. By this stage I could barely walk without pain. Every little knock or touch on my legs was incredibly tender. This made daily life quite difficult as I had four children, three of which were under five years old. Anyone with small children knows that they practically live around your ankles all day so they would often bump into my legs, which was excruciating for me. After explaining the symptoms to my local GP, he informed me that I would have to have a routine blood test. The blood disorder trait Alpha Thalassemia runs in my family so any link to this needed to be eliminated as soon as possible. Whilst we waited for the blood test results the doctor simply gave me some painkillers to help reduce my discomfort. They didn't help at all. A few days later the blood test results were returned and all links to the Thalassemia trait were clear. The results actually showed no abnormalities but the GP had to put it down to something. He explained that he could not be sure but settled on a diagnosis of the bacterial skin infection called Cellulites to which he could not source the origin. After a 10-day course of antibiotics the pain began to leave, eventually. Bruises stopped developing and I began to go through the healing process. As much as this sounds like a usual case of sickness that anyone could suffer, I believe it served as bait to get my mind off the task at hand.

During this time my children also began to experience vivid nightmares, in particular my eldest daughter and middle son. These two children had already displayed a similar gifting to me in the way of dreaming accurate events. It was not unusual for them to enter my room in the middle of the night crying and scared. Sometimes I would hear them screaming or crying from their bedrooms only to find that they had experienced such a nightmare. In response I dedicated more time to praying for Grandad and decided to add fasting to the equation. Those who had partnered with me in prayer earlier on also continued to pray for God's protection over my family. My husband's decorating business started picking up momentum and began to become very successful. Although this would seem like a positive thing, in actual fact it became incredibly burdensome. This was because the work piled in but no job ran smoothly. There always seemed to be complications, set backs or issues with the client which caused all sorts of stress and financial strain. Pressure was high in the household along with the hassle of constant mild infirmities in the family. I could do nothing else except cry out to God in prayer and keep reading and confessing 2 Peter 3:9 repeatedly. I just knew I could not give up – a life depended on it.

The diagnosis

Grandad had been diagnosed with diabetes back in 1990 but following a heart operation in the summer of 2007 it took a turn for the worse. I remembered that a heart operation was the procedure that was featured in my dream and considered that this may be the turning point that got the ball rolling. There is something quite surreal about a life event that mirrors what you have dreamt about previously. Surprisingly though, the heart operation was very successful and upon recovery Grandad seemed like his old self again. But shortly after this, his diabetic condition meant that he would now have to begin to rely on dialysis to stay healthy. Dialysis is a type of treatment that involves replicating a lot of the functions of the kidneys. It is usually used to treat cases of kidney failure - also known as end stage renal disease - which is when the kidneys have been severely damaged and lost almost all of their functioning capacity. Renal disease is common in long-standing diabetics and Grandad was not an exception. Relying on dialysis would mean three or four hospital appointments during the week in which he would be hooked up to a machine for a minimum of four to six hours. The doctors had a concern regarding whether his heart was strong enough to go through such an arduous procedure so frequently. They warned him that it would be risky as he could experience heart failure. Grandad could not bear the thought of being a slave to such a limiting process like dialysis and wanted to enjoy whatever life he had left to live without the burden of endless hospital visits. With this he made a decision to decline dialysis. The doctors stressed that the weight of this issue meant he was likely to only live another six months or so. Upon hearing this news I began to realize that what I had heard from God regarding his death was beginning to play out. I said nothing of my dream to him and his mind was set. Grandad stuck to his conviction regarding refusing treatment, undeterred by the doctor's essential talk of a death sentence. He actually seemed at peace with his choice and comfortable with the possibility that he may not see the end of the year. I am not sure whether the extended family really understood the full implications of this decision, partly because he seemed fairly well and was his usual chirpy self. At the same time all of this was going on I was surprised to find out that I was pregnant with my fifth child. This later proved to be a very significant part of God's plan for Grandad.

3

Mercy in our folly

*Let us then approach God's throne of grace with
confidence, so that we may receive mercy and find
grace to help us in our time of need.*
Hebrews 4:16 NIV

The distance to Grandad's house was only a
short walk from where I lived so I would visit him
once or twice a week. Since the decision to
decline the dialysis his health had slowly begun
to deteriorate. On the outside you could not
really tell because he seemed so happy, still
cracking the odd joke in his Jamaican patois.
Actually they were not really jokes but simply his
typical quirky comments. I found them funny
because of the character and attitude that came
along with them. But behind this he was
becoming less able to do some of the things he
would usually do. I remember he often liked to go
for a walk down to nearby Walworth Road. The
other grandchildren and I would frequently watch
him from the high kitchen window as he walked
down the landing to Westmoreland Road, which
was on his way. After a short while we would look
out the window again to see if he was coming

back. Come to think of it, the kitchen window was quite a significant part of the relationship us grandchildren had with Grandad. None of us owned keys to his maisonette where he lived with my Nan and where my mum and aunts grew up. So when we visited we would ring the bell and he would open the kitchen window and ask who it was. Once we revealed ourselves he would throw down the door keys so we could let ourselves in. If you learnt to catch that bunch of keys properly it secretly meant that you were a professional!

As time rolled by he stopped being the person who threw down the keys. It became apparent that his ability began to decline and Nanny could no longer care for him alone. Early dementia had truly begun to set in too. He was himself eighty percent of the time but then there was that twenty where he would just talk a lot of random chat, often about things that we had no clue about. Although it was odd, it was quite humorous at times, which helped the family cope with his condition. Like many diabetics Grandad had to take insulin daily and I would sit and watch my Nan or Mum help to administer it. Never did I pay detailed attention to when he needed it or get involved. Sometimes Nanny had to do things like pop to the shops or visit friends so would always get another family member to watch Grandad whilst she was out. It was not usual for her to ask me because of my heavy childcare schedule and due to the fact that I was expecting.

On one occasion she did ask me to stay with him. It was agreed that I would get to her house by 10am one morning and upon my arrival she would give me specific instructions on how to care for him. I had no reservations about looking after him and just intended to chill out. What could possibly go wrong? Unfortunately when I arrived, Nanny had already left. To be honest this was not a huge surprise to me. History proved that if you were not bang on time when it came to meeting up or visiting Nanny then she would not wait for you. I sighed when I realized that she had yet again rushed off. Always in a hurry, that was Nanny. No note had been written and she did not own a mobile phone so I could not call her with any queries. I had picked up a spare key from her the last time I visited and so I let myself in. Considering she would only be gone for a few hours I figured that not much could go wrong. Grandad and I chatted about this and that and his behaviour seemed perfectly normal – lovingly complaining about how Nanny was too fussy and that he did not need babysitting. I simply laughed, grateful to be spending some one on one time with him.

About an hour or so in and as lunchtime approached Grandad asked if he could have something to eat. Seeing as Nanny would be due back soon I simply told him that he would have to wait. It was unusual for Nanny to be later than she had said so I figured that it probably was not quite time for lunch. He calmly explained that Nanny always gave him his insulin around midday then his food shortly after to which I did have vague memories. Unsure, I was reluctant to fulfill his request and give him the insulin and a meal. He continued to insist it was time and that all my sisters had delivered it too. Throughout the months, my younger sisters had been involved in helping Nanny to care for him in a way I never had. Thinking about it, Nanny probably assumed I was familiar with his routine as I had been around so often. There was nothing abnormal about the way that Grandad was communicating to me. One of the great myths about dementia is that the sufferer will seem crazy. I guess that is only the case if they are actually speaking words or sentences that make no sense. He seemed fine and did not appear to be suffering from the slight dementia we had begun to experience but in my hesitancy I called my mum to find out what was the best thing to do. Unable to reach her I did what I would later regret and panicked with what to do. If you want to hear the Holy Spirit speak to you when faced with a dilemma the worst thing you can do is panic! In this state I could not even hear the voice of God if indeed He was speaking (and for the record I believe He was). I did not even ask for help. In the past I have asked the Holy Spirit many questions and more often than not I receive an answer. Either "Yes", "No", "Not yet" or "Never you mind". These answers have sometimes been accompanied with some sort of explanation but not always. I eventually made the decision to administer the insulin. This proved to be a horrific mistake although in that moment I did not know it. Grandad calmly packed the instruments away and sat to wait for Nanny to return. Before long Nanny came back and nearly killed me when I told her what I had done. If she had not returned and given him something to eat quickly I would have been faced with a completely different level of decision-making. Soon Grandad would have begun to experience a range of reactions including paleness, shaking, rapid heartbeat and blurred vision. Further down the line he could have faced a loss of consciousness and convulsions. With his already weak heart, this could have proven fatal.

That day I left feeling like a total idiot. How could I have been so stupid? Even now when I recall the events it is just embarrassing. I felt terrible, vowing to never be trusted to look after Grandad again, wallowing in self-pity. For the next few days I simply felt depressed and it took about four weeks for me to feel at peace with this grave mistake. I knew I had officially blown it, unqualified myself to be part of God's plan for Grandad. I found it difficult to even talk to God about it in prayer. So ashamed that I could have been so foolish to think I knew what I was doing or that the consequences would not be bad. When I finally mustered the courage to vocally bring it to God I simply asked Him if He would use someone else because surely I could not be trusted. But after spending a lot of time in His presence I got back to the mission and refocussed. If not for God, things could have been much worse and Grandad could have died prematurely because of my folly. Thank God for his mercy.

4

Our mini celebration

*For God so loved the world that He gave His one
and only Son, that whoever believes in Him shall
not perish but have eternal life.*
John 3:16 NIV

After several delays, nervous professionals and
nearly fifty minutes of carefully investigating my
baby during a scan, the senior consultant
stopped and looked at Harold and me. We looked
first at each other then at the consultant and
wondered what was going on. At an appointment
a few weeks before there was a horrendous mix
up with myself and another mother following a
routine scan. I was asked to confirm what
illnesses and conditions ran in my family then
was casually told by the doctor that my baby had
a high chance of having Down's syndrome. This
conversation remains a blur so I cannot
remember the actual details of how they arrived
at this prognosis but I remember feeling a little
numb at hearing the news and shocked at how it
so comfortably rolled off the tongue of the doctor.
A few moments later I was told (again in a very

relaxed manner) that there had been a mistake and in actual fact, the Down's syndrome news was meant for another mother. I was stunned at how such an insensitive mistake could have been made but felt both relief and sympathy for the other party.

But this time the look on the consultant's face was different. After what seemed like a lot of back and forth questioning he asked us whether heart disease ran in the family. My mind cast back to the mix up a few weeks earlier. He explained that he had found a ventricular septal defect (a hole) in our baby's tiny heart and that this type of defect occurs in as little as two to six babies per 1000 births. Although it was beating normally, he did have some cause for concern and recommended another scan in a few months time. There was a chance if the hole did not close whilst the baby was inside the womb that heart surgery would be necessary to repair it. As I listened intently he continued to explain a small risk of long term effects throughout her life in the form of a heart murmur and possible cardiac difficulties if surgery didn't go ahead. As concerned as I felt, I trusted God enough to know that this had to be part of a great testimony that would be played out. As Harold and I left hospital, I pondered how much trouble the enemy had gone through to stop me from praying and obeying God.

As the weeks moved on I found it increasingly necessary to press into God and spend time with Him every day. I could not afford to make another wrong move. Grandad was now suffering the effects of dementia at least forty percent of the time. I felt as though time was running out and that it was drawing near for the fundamental chat to present the gospel to him. Consumed with all of this helped to keep my mind off of the worry I was prone to regarding the baby's heart. I arranged to visit Grandad the following week whilst Nanny was out doing her running around at which I would seriously talk to him about God. I urged her not to leave before I arrived and made sure he had eaten already.

November came so quickly and Nanny left not long after I turned up at the flat. I decided not to hesitate, turned to Grandad and simply told him the truth. With a peace and confidence I had not felt until now, I explained to him that he was going to die whether he liked it or not and that heaven and hell were very real places, one of which he would end up in. To some this may sound like I was trying to scare him but I honestly wasn't thinking about that. In my mind we were running out of time and dancing around the issue was not going to help. I needed to be direct but loving, that's how God is with us. I told him that Jesus had paid the price for him if he would acknowledge his sin before God and accept His free gift of eternal life. It was his choice. He nodded as I communicated all of this to him, bowing his head and looking at me interchangeably. I felt I had done all that I could and it was God that needed to do the rest. The next few minutes were filled with Grandad asking me what he needed to do, confessing his sins and praying the sinners' prayer with me. This was followed by a mini celebration between the two of us. We took photos using my mobile phone as we laughed and chatted. Although we had shared many moments together, none was quite like this one. I sang a song of praise with Grandad clapping along and what seemed like a few moments later, Nanny returned. She hadn't a clue why we were so chuffed but was happy all had run smoothly this time round. I got ready to leave, feeling that all the pressure and fighting over the last year was so worth it. I kissed Grandad on the cheek as usual before leaving and sang all the way home. If I could have run I would have but my growing bump was proving quite tiresome. At this point I felt ready to let Grandad die because I knew he would be with God after his departure. It was a very strange feeling.

5

The last days

*"In the last day, God says, I will pour out my spirit
on all people. Your sons and daughters will
prophesy, your young men will see visions, your
old men will dream dreams."*
Ecclesiastes 3:1 NIV

I remember the bright blue paint of the walls in
Nanny and Grandad's home. It was so bright; in
fact it was too bright. Every few years Grandad
would get out a tin of identical blue paint and
redo the walls. I can recall a year when he
discovered a dead mouse along one of the
skirting boards and simply painted it blue to
match everything else! The family and I laughed
at this story for years. Lately every time I entered
that flat I would remember such a story, one that
involved Grandad's spritely character. All the
things I was so used to him doing gradually
stopped. He would often watch darts or
Brookside on his tiny black and white television
in the living room if Nanny was watching
something more important like Countdown or
Fifteen to one. Playing his reggae LP's for hours,

having a secret cigarette or fumbling around in his upstairs storage cupboard was no longer the norm. One thing he always did was look out of the window, or out the back over the balcony. He would just stand and look out. Thinking. I often wondered what went through his mind.

Grandad got very ill as the toxins took over his body and a decision was made to admit him into a hospice as doctors were sure he had only a few weeks left at the most. The family gathered round to say their goodbyes. Although he visited with the rest of us, I was struck by a confidence my brother Michael had. He was not convinced that Grandad was on his last legs just yet. To my surprise he was right and the time Grandad spent in the hospice actually saw him improve greatly. He did not look like a man who was going to keel over any minute, but a man who was full of everything to live for. Soon the decision was made to send him back home.

None of us expected it but Christmas came and went and Grandad was still with us. As much as I was happy about this, it was weird. I was ready to let Grandad go but it seemed like God wasn't. I wondered what he was holding out for now that the mission was accomplished. Dementia was still prevalent and the family gathered round to take turns to care for him. Visits to the toilet and basic living had become difficult on an independent level. Due to the increasing number of demands that his health presented, palliative care nurses had also joined us in helping Nanny to care for him. Throughout this time of both normalcy and dementia Grandad would talk about heaven a lot. He would speak of the "place" he was going to and asked when we would join him. He would talk about Jesus coming to get him and was assured that he was destined for an eternity with God. Another subject that he would ask about a lot was the arrival of a baby. He never mentioned this baby's name but would simply ask if she was here yet. Seeing as I was expecting at the time, naturally family members would ask whether it was my baby he was referring to but he never answered.

Grandad was no longer able to venture to the upstairs of the house so remained confined to the downstairs bedroom. This again was very abnormal because you would rarely find Grandad in the lower part of the home let alone the bedroom unless he was going to bed at night. Now it was likely to be his permanent residence. But he had a strange surge of energy on January 2nd 2008 and he managed it up the stairs for a special celebration. The entire family made an effort to attend and celebrate his 79th birthday along with my own dad who shared this special day with him. Everyone was amazed with this newfound strength but we basked in his presence and had fun taking lots of family photos. It was a really special time together and looking back, I think we all knew that this would be his last birthday celebration. Little did we know that this would actually be his last time upstairs too and that never again would we see him as smiley and energetic.

He became confined to the bed again eventually not being able to get up unaided for anything. He stopped talking and slept more and more until it became constant. His breathing laboured heavily as days went by without him waking up even once. Only the clicking sound of the morphine being released into his body every now and again and the heavy breathing could be heard. I wondered what consumed his thoughts and dreams as he lay there, thinking that he was probably spending some time conversing with God. The time was drawing near for him to go, I could just tell. I felt upset because due to my progressing pregnancy I could not visit as much. Prayer continued and God would lay scriptures on my heart to share with Grandad that I was unable to give him. It was not good enough for me to call on the phone to deliver them, I had to be there. I later found out that some of the very scriptures God gave me were being read to him by one of the palliative care nurses, who happened to be a Christian. Mabel was her name and I never got a chance to communicate very much with her or thank her. Prior to this, Nanny had also spent time telling him to make peace with God before he died.

Another scan showed that my baby still had the heart defect and it was no smaller. Although doctors expected the hole to be closed by the time she was born it was agreed that a home birth would not be an option. It was also recommended that she would need to be scanned again shortly after birth just to make sure it had closed. The consultants gave me a bunch of leaflets which outlined the condition and possible complications that could occur after the birth. I did not really consider these implications properly instead fixed my mind on God and trusted that there must be a plan to all of this.

6

The final visit

There is a time for everything, and a season for every activity under heaven
Ecclesiastes 3:1 NIV

In the last week of January doctors were sure that Grandad would not survive beyond the coming weekend and urged the family to say their goodbyes again. This time it was very different from months before at the hospice. By now Grandad had lost so much weight and had been in a deep sleep for weeks. He could no longer move and had not opened his eyes; however we were convinced he could hear us. So we would all take it in turns to sit and speak with him. I have never asked my siblings and cousins what they chose to say to Grandad. My guess is that we all had something uniquely special to communicate even if we chose to use no words. I decided to visit on the Friday because I had a very busy weekend ahead. My baby shower had been arranged to take place on the Saturday and there were a few things to do. In the evening after Harold came home from work I walked round to

41

the house still not really thinking that this could be the last time I would see him.

It was a bit busy when I arrived as family members came and went. Strangely there were no palliative care nurses present, it had turned out that there was a misunderstanding, which meant nobody had been booked. My mum was very angry about this mix up and as she made various phone calls to try and rectify the situation I thought I would take the opportunity to catch up on a bit of television. I watched a few programmes but didn't really take much of the information in. The house felt different.

After an hour or so, I ventured downstairs to see how Grandad was fairing. It was strange being with him and I half expected him to wake up and say my name in his funny Jamaican Patois "Nikla" as was usual. But he didn't. Somehow though, in that moment I felt like his favourite grandchild. In reality he had no favourites but if you ask the other grandchildren they all would probably say that it was them. He did not have to say anything; I just knew in my heart that he loved me. We all knew his time was drawing near as I whispered scriptures and caring words in his ear. He had a funny smell about him that I do not think I will ever forget. It was not a horrible one but different to what you might expect of one who had been bedridden for a while. When a baby is born they have what my sisters and I call "that newborn baby smell". It is just new. Grandad had that same kind of smell, one that I cannot accurately describe. Perhaps, like the smell at birth it was somehow the smell of death.

My dad came in shortly afterwards asking Grandad to hold on and not give up the fight just yet. I guess he was dealing with the inevitability of losing Grandad in his own way. He too was close to Grandad in an exceptional way. I think in some respect he was closer to him than his own father and wondered how his birthdays would be different after he had gone. I got quite angry with him telling Grandad to hold on so told him off a little bit. I knew that all Grandad wanted to do was die as he had spoken about it for weeks and wondered what was taking so long. He had given his life to Jesus Christ and was destined for eternity with Him so he didn't see the point of sticking around. I imagined that if Grandad could talk he would probably tell Daddy to shut up and we would all laugh. I turned to

The Altar

Grandad and whispered what would be my last
words:

*"Don't listen to Daddy Grandad. It is almost done.
Your time will soon come and this will all be over.
It soon done, it soon done."*

I told him that I loved him and then left to go
home. After being on the phone for some time my
mum confirmed that nobody from the palliative
care team was coming so she and my sister
would stay over with Nanny and do shifts to
watch Grandad. She was a little worried that she
would not know what to do if he died in the
night. I was sure she would be fine even under
the circumstances as she always handled these
unexpected events with ease. To be honest, my
mum should have been a nurse because she is
just naturally good at looking after people and
remaining calm in testing situations.

Daddy gave me a lift home in the car as it was
after midnight by the time I was leaving. I entered
my house to find Harold still awake and he asked
me how things went. I had no intention of going
to bed because I wanted to talk about everything
but as I began talking I suddenly felt very unwell.

A sickly feeling that I couldn't quite put my finger on came over me. It was just a strange sense of weakness. I decided to pack the things I needed for childbirth into my hospital bag as I had been putting it off for months and then climbed into bed. But at about 02:30 I woke up with labour pains knowing full well that my baby was getting ready to be born. I decided not to wake Harold straight away because he needed to get some sleep after only going to bed an hour or so before. I thought I would have a bath to help me relax a bit then wake him after. But things progressed much quicker than I expected and after being in the bath for about ten minutes the contractions were too intense to deal with by myself. After calling Harold from upstairs he came to help me. Within the next thirty minutes an emergency operator was on the phone instructing Harold on how to deliver the baby. My sister whom we had called minutes before had left my mum and granddad to look after my children whilst I went to the hospital. I told her off because she ran all the way from Nanny's house alone in the dark, putting herself at risk. I actually didn't make it to the hospital and my fifth baby made her entrance into the world seconds after two ambulance crews and my dad arrived. I was incredibly shocked to see the crowd that had gathered including two of my children who had been woken by all the extra visitors. Against the recommendations of the doctors I had delivered at home as there had not been enough time to get into the ambulance.

About twenty minutes after my new daughter was born my mum called to congratulate me. During the short phone call I discovered that something quite incredible had occurred. A message was sent to Mum to tell her that I was in labour. On receiving this message she entered Grandad's room and shared the news with him. As she told him the baby was on its way Grandad responded with breathing out his last breath and finally left this earth. He died minutes before Michaela was born although the time of his pronounced death matched the exact time of her birth. 04:20am. Several hours later the ambulance drove us to the hospital so they could check on the condition of Michaela's heart and no sooner had we arrived, they whisked her off for a scan. As I watched her squirming due to the coldness of the instrument they were using; I wondered what they would find. Report came back that the heart defect was still present and was no smaller. They advised Harold and I that they would have to scan her heart every month to check if it was changing. There was a high chance that it would close on its own and heart surgery would be considered if it did not. In the meantime she would live a normal life but we were again informed of concerning signs to look for in her breathing. If we were anxious about her at all then we were to take her to see a GP. After a quick examination from the Pediatrician I was allowed to take Michaela back home.

7

Farewell

He who testifies to these things says, "Yes. I am coming soon" Amen. Come, Lord Jesus
Revelation 22:20 NIV

The next few days were all a blur to me. In the back of my mind I knew my family were grieving together and were making funeral arrangements. I did not get to visit them, attend the wake, known in the West Indies as a "Nine Night" or view Grandad's body at the undertakers. As happy and blessed as I felt to have my new daughter I also felt incredibly detached from the rest of the family. I was used to being involved in family affairs and wanted to share the unity that I know they all had at this time. I did not feel sad or distraught that Grandad was gone and did not cry but I knew that everyone else would be very upset. I thought a lot about my brother and how he was fairing, as they were always incredibly close and had a mutual passion for music. The fact that I was not upset was all a bit confusing for me as I thought I should have been. I had never suffered such a close and personal bereavement so surely I should be crying? Looking back I know that having a baby and losing a relative at the same time just meant that I could not possibly process the entire situation.

We buried Grandad's body less than two weeks later and I still did not cry. The morning came and I got myself ready to walk the short walk to the flat where the family were gathering and leaving in the hearses. Many of the females in the family were in dark glasses and I knew that underneath them were already teary, exhausted eyes from the crying. I remember everyone looking so well dressed, somehow more so than usual. I looked at the casket in the hearse and remembered that Grandad had always said that he did not want to be drawn by a horse and carriage when he died. I never actually knew why that was. Several relatives asked me if I was okay somehow suspecting that I might have not processed everything properly. They would be right. We made our way to the church where Nanny worshipped for decades and so many family events had been celebrated. My parents had got married there; I was a bridesmaid at an Aunt's wedding, confirmations, birthdays, generations of christenings and my own wedding reception had all been memorable family moments there. But today was a very different day. We were all going there dressed in black to say goodbye to Grandad. For the first time I began to feel sad that he was gone. I remember thinking that when I die I did not want people wearing black. Seeing so many people in the dark clothing does something to you emotionally. It definitely added to the grief and made things seem a lot worse. Even though I knew Grandad was with God it was still an upsetting event. I asked my husband why death is always so difficult to comprehend. Human beings have been dying every day for centuries, surely by now we should be used to it? But he told me that the reason why we will never be able to fully understand it is because it was never supposed to happen. It was never God's plan for us to experience death. So although I was sad I had a relief and joy in my heart that I was sure of Grandad's destination. At the start of the service I was the first family member to do a scripture reading. I am not sure whose bright idea this was but I mustered up the courage to proceed. Naturally I was nervous but knew it was something that was important. I stumbled all the way through a difficult King James Version that had been provided for me and did not do the beauty of the scripture any justice. Then the next hour or so was filled with memories of Grandad's life, weeping from loved ones and the final goodbyes.

The memories of the journey to the cemetery are a bit misty. What I do remember being was exhausted, after all it was the first real outing since having the baby. There is something about seeing the casket lowered into the ground and covered with soil that really says things are final. A strange desire to jump into the hole felt so wrong but powerfully present regardless. It is such a ridiculous notion that it puts into perspective the fact that this loved one has gone somewhere that we cannot go. It was over, Grandad had been buried and his years in this life were complete. He had taken nothing with him. Nothing. We were all left behind, his belongings, all the things he had held dear remained for us to sort out. The journey of the last two years began to make sense and I was able to see how God had truly moved throughout that whole time. It was his plan from the beginning to see Grandad saved and that meant having to speak to me about it years before. I wondered if it was a good or bad thing that God required so much time, probably needing to take into account all my errors. But I guess that did not really matter now. He was with God and in that respect His will had been done.

As planned, Michaela was scanned every month after this. With each appointment I was reminded of the journey we had just embarked upon over the last two years. I later found out that Grandad's youngest daughter had been born with the same heart defect and that Grandad himself had always had an irregular heartbeat. It appeared that hearts were a bit of a theme in this story somehow and that God was able to use it to illustrate how much we all mean to Him. Thankfully on July 24th 2008 the hole in Michaela's heart finally closed in an extraordinary way. Upon scanning, it looked as though someone had simply covered the hole with a plaster rather than it being filled. It was quite comical to look at and the doctors were a bit bemused at how it had healed in this way. I think that God likes to leave us with little reminders that He had a hand in working things out just in case we forget. Michaela was signed off and given the all clear.

For months, years and until today I contemplate all the details of this testimony. When I look at Michaela I think of what happened with saving Grandad instantly. I am constantly reminded of God's goodness, sovereignty and greatness. And although I have cried and grieved in my own unique way I cannot help but get excited about the day I will see Grandad again.

-x-

Prayer

Lord I thank you so much for the awesome privilege of knowing you. Thank you for saving Grandad because of your unfailing love for him. Thank you for your commitment to our love relationship and for never giving up on me. You continue to amaze me as I learn more about you. I want to know you intimately and glorify your name through my life. I thank you that you called me to yourself despite my flawed, sinful nature, for your protection and blessings.

Lord will you remove the veil from the eyes of those who are still in darkness. It is your desire to see them redeemed. Help me to not only be called but to continually walk in obedience to your leading.

I love you.

Nichola

Appendix 1

Dream interpretation: The basics

There are a vast number of information texts on how to interpret dreams. Frankly speaking, you can find some that are full of rubbish and of no help at all. The scriptures of the Bible should form the basis of how to go about interpreting and therefore any method or approach that violates this truth should be avoided. In this section I will share some of the basics I have learnt that helped me start the process of understanding my dreams. I am by no means an expert on the subject and am only sharing what I have practised over the years and what has worked for me.

Remember that God is the one whom I ultimately rely on to receive clarity on any dream I have, but also note that not all dreams come from Him. If you want to find out more information, I recommend reading a book called "Dreams and Visions" By Jane Hamon as a starting point.

The following interpretation guidelines are things that have helped me *personally* to get to the bottom of my dreams and their origins. They may also be useful for you if you are a believer in Jesus, the risen saviour of the Bible and follow the blueprint for life found in the scriptures.

There are two habits I have developed that help me to pinpoint what my dreams may be about and make for easy referencing:

Keep a journal. At the start of every year I purchase an A4 page-a-day diary that I use to keep accounts of my dreams. This may be more than you need if you are just starting out. When I first began the habit of journaling I used an A5 size but as the years have gone on I have found the need to purchase something bigger. Even now, I am limited in how much I can write so often have extra bits of paper stuck inside. I will soon need to think of something else. I prefer diaries instead of notebooks because they come with the dates already printed in them. When I have a dream all I need to do is record it onto the page with that date. Journaling is a great way to express thoughts and feelings about life, relationships and deep issues of the soul and spirit. It promotes reflection, can help to identify my character strengths and weaknesses, is therapeutic and identifies patterns of increased or decreased frequency of dreams. I do not make an entry every single day but as often as I can to record my thoughts, prayers and anything the Lord communicates to me.

Be familiar with how your mind and body responds to things. If I watch certain movies or eat certain foods before going to sleep, this can cause me to experience dreams of a particular nature. For example: A heavy meal after 9pm often triggers a series of small dreams that make no sense. They simply jump around a lot with no real purpose to them. If I go to bed mad at my husband it will always result in an attacking dream of a demonic nature. These dreams act as a stark reminder of the danger of unforgiveness in my heart. I avoid having to encounter these dreams as much as I can. If I am overtired or burnt out I usually fail to remember any dream the instant I wake up. It is very challenging to recall these later. As a habit I do not watch horror or any movies with strong occult messages. If I do, I open myself up to graphic dreams that can be tremendously hideous and often very scary. I am very serious about guarding my heart against these things. In addition, during particularly stressful periods in my life, I simply don't dream at all as my mind is consumed with other things. It is necessary for me to get back to a place of peace in order to hear from God clearly.

Some general guidelines of interpretation:

Above all else, the first thing to do following a dream is to **WRITE IT DOWN**. This step should not be skipped. If you fail to write it down and rely solely on your memory to help you, this is a sure way to end up with nothing at all. Sometimes within a few minutes, details of the dream begin to fade away so always keep a pen and journal very near your bed (the closer the better). In addition to writing down the content make a note of any **STRONG FEELINGS** you may have. It may be helpful to give your dream a **TITLE**.

Feel free to **DRAW PICTURES** as sometimes this helps to capture the essence of the dream in more detail. Try to represent any images that carried significance in the form of a drawing. You could also record your dream in the form of a labelled diagram or flowchart. Once you have the dream down on paper ask yourself some **QUESTIONS**. What is my dream about? Is there a subject matter? Could this be about me or someone else? Am I in the dream? If so, where? Doing what? Try to identify the main focus. Then **REVIEW** all the information and ask God to help you understand. You may gain understanding very quickly, later that day or maybe weeks or months later. I believe it is okay to ask a Pastor, Mentor or someone who you trust and respect spiritually to give their reflection of your dream but try not to do this too early as sometimes it can cloud your judgement. I would also, recommend refraining from using extensive biblical dream symbolism dictionaries. They can be used as tools to aide you in your dream interpretation but should no way be a substitute for listening to the Holy Spirit. Take some time to seek the answer for yourself and continue to keep notes of your reflections and as clarity is received.

The Altar

Summary

1. Keep a Journal

2. Be familiar with how your mind and body responds to things

3. Following a dream, get up (and out of bed if necessary)

4. Write down an account of the dream including strong feelings

5. Add diagrams or drawings if needed - the more detailed, the better

6. Ask yourself some relevant questions and try your best to answer them

7. Review all your information asking God to help you gain understanding. Note anything that you think or feel he says to you

8. Re-read and continue to reflect, making written notes along the way

I hope you have found the information contained in this book useful.

Happy dreaming!

Recommended reading

Dreams and Visions
Jane Hamon

Some dreams found in the Bible:

Genesis 20:3-7
In the story of Abraham and Sarah, Abimelech is warned against taking Sarah from Abraham.

Genesis 40:5-23
Joseph interprets dreams in prison

Daniel 4:2-25
Daniel interprets King Nebuchadnezzar's dream

Matt. 1:20
Joseph receives instruction to go ahead and marry Mary

Matt 27:19
The Wife of Pilate suffers in a dream as a warning not to crucify Jesus

Sidney George Grey
2nd January 1929 – 2nd February 2008

Made in the USA
Charleston, SC
18 February 2015